DAMIAN LILLARD

Rapper, Philanthropist, and Basketball Superstar

Norman D. Smith

CONTENTS

PRESENTATION

In the powerful universe of elite athletics, hardly any figures epitomize the substance of adaptability and greatness as flawlessly as Damian Lillard. Past the resonating reverberations of b-ball fields, Lillard's story rises above the limits of the hardwood, laying out a picture of a multi-layered ability — a rapper, donor, and b-ball hotshot. This book tries to unwind the layers of a man whose excursion from the coarse roads of Oakland to the excellent phases of the NBA has been downright unprecedented.

As the heartbeat of the Portland Pioneers, Lillard has carved his name into the records of ball history with a mark style that joins unflinching assurance, unmatched expertise, and a resolute quiet notwithstanding pressure. "Woman Time" isn't simply an expression; it's a demonstration of Lillard's capacity to immediately jump all over the opportunity, conveying grasp exhibitions that have turned into the stuff of legend.

However, there's something else to Damian Lillard besides the accuracy of his three-pointers and the artfulness of his court vision. In the domain of music, he changes into Woman D.O.L.L.A., a scholar who explores the beats with a similar effortlessness he shows on the court. His rhymes reverberation the real factors of his childhood, the difficulties confronted, and the victories celebrated. The combination of ball and hip-bounce turns into an exceptional focal point through which we investigate the cooperative energy of Lillard's interests.

Past the spotlight, Lillard stands tall as a guide of generosity, utilizing his foundation to impact positive change. From drives supporting oppressed networks to backing for civil rights, he channels his impact towards having an enduring effect off the court. The strings of his humanitarian embroidery wind through the story, uncovering a pledge to making an inheritance that reaches out a long ways past the bounds of b-ball fields.

Go along with us on an excursion through the ups and downs, the beats and bounce back, as we dive into the convincing story of Damian Lillard — a man who resists order, consistently mixing the universes of sports, music, and generosity. Through the pages of this book, find the quintessence of the rapper, humanitarian, and b-ball whiz, and reveal the mosaic of a day to day existence inhabited the crossing point of enthusiasm and reason.

INTRODUCING DAMIAN LILLARD

Damian Lamonte Ollie "Woman" Lillard Sr. (conceived July 15, 1990) is an American expert b-ball player for the Milwaukee Bucks of the Public B-ball Affiliation (NBA). He played school b-ball for the Weber State Wildcats and procured third-group All-American distinctions in 2012. Subsequent to being chosen by the Portland Pioneers with the 6th generally speaking pick in the 2012 NBA draft, Lillard was collectively casted a ballot the NBA The latest phenom. Nicknamed Lady Time for his set of experiences of making big cheeses in the grasp, he has gotten seven NBA Top pick and seven All-NBA Group choices, the main player in Pioneers establishment history to do as such. In October 2021, Lillard was respected as one of the association's most prominent players ever by being named to the NBA 75th Commemoration Group. He likewise won a gold decoration on the 2020 U.S. Olympic group in Tokyo.

Damian Lillard

Lillard with the Portland Pioneers in 2021

No. 0 - Milwaukee Bucks

Position

Point watch

Association

NBA

Individual data

Conceived

July 15, 1990 (age 33)

Oakland, California, U.S.

Recorded level

6 ft 2 in (1.88 m)

Recorded weight

195 lb (88 kg)

Vocation data

Secondary school

Arroyo

(San Lorenzo, California)

St. Joseph Notre Lady

(Alameda, California)

Oakland

(Oakland, California)

School

Weber State (2008-2012)

NBA draft

2012: first round, sixth by and large pick

Chosen by the Portland Pioneers

Playing vocation

2012-present

Vocation history

2012-2023

Portland Pioneers

2023-present

Milwaukee Bucks

Profession features and grants

7× NBA Elite player (2014, 2015, 2018-2021, 2023)

All-NBA First Group (2018)

4× All-NBA Second Group (2016, 2019-2021)

2× All-NBA Third Group (2014, 2023)

NBA The new hotness (2013)

NBA All-New kid on the block First Group (2013)

NBA 75th Commemoration Group

NBA Partner of the Year (2021)

NBA Three-Point Challenge champion (2023)

Third-group All-American - AP, NABC (2012)

2× Large Sky Player of the Year (2010, 2012)

Large Sky Green bean of the Year (2009)

3× First-group All-Large Sky (2009, 2010, 2012)

No. 1 resigned by Weber State Wildcats

Details Alter this at Wikidata at NBA.com

Details Alter this at Wikidata at B-ball Reference.com

Awards

Men's b-ball

Addressing the US

Olympic Games

Gold award - first place   2020 Tokyo   Team

Utilizing the stage name Lady D.O.L.L.A., Lillard has delighted in moderate accomplishment as a rapper. His most memorable studio collection, The Letter O (2016), graphed on the Announcement 200, while his second and third collections, Affirmed (2017) and Huge D.O.L.L.A. (2019), put on the non mainstream graphs. In 2021, he delivered a fourth collection, Different On Levels The Ruler Permitted.

HIGH SCHOOL PROFESSION

Lillard started his secondary school profession at Arroyo Secondary School in San Lorenzo, California, and joined the varsity beginning setup as a 5 ft 5 in (1.65 m) green bean. He tried to move when his mentor didn't get back to the group. For his sophomore year, Lillard moved to St. Once more joseph Notre Woman Secondary School in Alameda, California, the very tuition based school that had created previous NBA point watch Jason Kidd; however by the end of the year, an absence of playing time provoked Lillard to move schools. He proceeded to play for mentor Orlando Watkins at Oakland Secondary School, where he was First Group

All-Association his lesser and senior years. Over his lesser mission, Lillard found the middle value of 19.4 focuses an evening. As a senior, he found the middle value of 22.4 places and 5.2 helps per game while driving the Oakland Wildcats to a 23-9 record.

Viewed exclusively as a two-star prospect by Rivals.com, Lillard was not vigorously selected out of secondary school, yet he acknowledged a grant proposition to play for Weber Express, a Major Sky Meeting program in Ogden, Utah. As per Lillard, Weber State was the primary school b-ball program to show any interest in him when lead trainer Randy Rahe appeared face to face to watch Lillard play a game in

Texas during his lesser year of secondary school. Lillard decided to go to Weber State in Utah to some extent since he needed to move away from his rough Oakland area. He had gotten contending offers from schools including Wichita State, Holy person Mary's and San Diego State.

US school sports enlisting data for secondary school competitors

Name Hometown   High school/college Height WeightCommit date

Damian Lillard

PG   Oakland, California   Oakland High 6 ft 0 in (1.83 m)   165 lb (75 kg)Sep 26, 2007

Enlisting star evaluations: Scout:2/5 stars Rivals:2/5 stars 247Sports:3/5 stars ESPN grade: 85

By and large enrolling rankings: Scout: 100 (PG) ESPN: 48 (PG)

Note: Generally speaking, Scout, Adversaries, 247Sports, and ESPN might struggle in their postings of level and weight.

In these cases, the normal was taken. ESPN grades are on a 100-point scale.

Sources:

"2008 Weber State School B-ball Group Enrolling Possibilities". Scout.com. Filed from the first on February 27, 2017. Recovered February 27, 2017.

"Weber State Wildcats 2008 Player Commits". ESPN.com. Filed from the first on February 27, 2017. Recovered February 27, 2017.

"Scout.com Group Selecting Rankings". Scout.com. Recovered February 27, 2017.

"2008 Group Positioning". Rivals.com. Recovered February 27, 2017.

SCHOOL VOCATION

As a green bean at Weber State, Lillard found the middle value of 11.5 focuses per game and was named the Huge Sky Gathering Rookie of the Year and first-group All-Large Sky. In his sophomore year, he raised his scoring normal to 19.9 focuses per game and drove the Wildcats to the meeting title. Toward the finish of the time, Lillard was named Huge Sky Player of the Year as well as noteworthy notice All-American by the Related Press.

In 2010-11, Lillard drove the Huge Sky in scoring with 19.7 focuses per challenge prior to experiencing a foot injury ten games into the season that constrained him to take a clinical redshirt and sidelined him until the end of the year.

As a redshirt junior, Lillard found the middle value of 24.5 places and drove the country in scoring all through a large portion of the year yet wound up completing second to Oakland College's Reggie Hamilton. On December 3, 2011, against San Jose State, Lillard scored a school vocation high 41 focuses, including a game-securing three-guide play toward give Weber Express a 91-89 twofold extra time win. Toward the year's end, he was named to his third first-group all-meeting choice and won his second

Huge Sky Player of the Year grant. Lillard was likewise a finalist for the Bounce Cousy Grant.

Generally viewed as the top point watch prospect in the country, Lillard chose to skirt his senior season to enter the 2012 NBA draft. He completed his school vocation as the No. 2 scorer in Weber State history (1,934 focuses) and the No. 5 scorer in Enormous Sky history.

He finished his certification in proficient deals from Weber State College in May 2015.

PROFICIENT VOCATION

Portland Pioneers (2012-2023)

2012-13 season: The new hotness

Lillard endeavors a leap shot over Draymond Green with the Pioneers in January 2013.

Lillard was chosen with the 6th in general pick in the 2012 NBA draft by the Portland Pioneers. In the season opener against the Los Angeles Lakers on October 31, Lillard recorded 23 focuses and 11 helps to join Oscar Robertson and Allen Iverson as the main players in NBA history with no less than 20 places and 10 aids their NBA debut. Moreover, his 11 helps were the most by a NBA tenderfoot in his most memorable game since Jason Kidd (11) in 1994, and the most ridiculously ever by a Pioneer in his NBA debut. Lillard made a vocation high 15 field objectives and a Pioneer new kid on the block record seven 3-pointers on January 11 against the Brilliant State Champions, where he got done with 37 focuses, six bounce back, and four helps. He turned into the principal Pioneer to win an occasion at the NBA Top pick End of the week, winning the Abilities Challenge. He likewise took part in the Rising Stars Challenge during Elite player end of the week and wrapped up with 18 places, three bounce back and five aids a game-high 28 minutes. Lillard turned into the main NBA freshman to record 35 focuses, nine helps and no turnovers in a game since turnovers turned into a detail in 1978-79 against the San Antonio Spikes on Walk 8. On April 10 against the Lakers, Lillard scored a season-high 38 focuses. He acquired Western Gathering Tenderfoot of the Month praises for each month, becoming one of only eight players to clear NBA Newbie of the Month respects since the debut grant in 1981-82. He completed fifth in the NBA in 3-pointers made, twelfth in focuses per game, tied for sixteenth in helps per game and tied for 23rd in free toss rate. He was one of 10 NBA players to score 1,500 focuses, and he drove all youngsters in scoring (19.0 ppg), helps (6.5 apg), field objectives (553) and free tosses (271).

With midpoints of 19.0 places, 3.1 bounce back, 6.5 helps, 0.90 takes, and 38.6 minutes in 82 games (all beginning), Lillard not just guaranteed the NBA The new hotness Grant yet joined Blake Griffin (2011), David Robinson (1990), and Ralph Sampson (1984) as the main consistent victors. He likewise joined Oscar Robertson and Allen Iverson as the main newbies in NBA history to count more than 1,500 focuses and 500 helps for a season. Lillard turned into the fourth Pioneer in establishment history to win NBA The latest phenom respects and one of two to at any point complete a season with something like 1,500 focuses and 500 helps (the other being Clyde Drexler in 1986-87 and 1991-92). Among different qualifications, he broke the untouched NBA newbie record for 3-pointers in a season (185), outperforming Stephen Curry's 166 three-pointers in 2009-10; turned into the Portland establishment pioneer for most 3-point field objectives in a season, breaking Damon Stoudamire's record of 181 of every 2004-05; and turned into the first new kid on the block to lead the NBA in quite a while played (3,167) since Elvin Hayes in 1968-69.

2013-14 season: First Top pick and All-NBA choice

In the season opener on October 30, Lillard scored 32 focuses against the Phoenix Suns. He had a second 32-point exertion on December 7 against the Dallas Dissidents. On December 17, he had 36 focuses, 10 helps, and eight bounce back against the Cleveland Cavaliers. The next day, he had a second consecutive 36-point exertion against the Minnesota Timberwolves. On January 7, in a 123-119 misfortune to the Sacramento Rulers, Lillard scored a vocation high 41 focuses, remembering 26 for the final quarter to break Portland's establishment record for most places in any quarter. On February 7, he had a 38-point exertion against the Indiana Pacers. During Top pick end of the week, Lillard turned into the primary player in NBA history to participate in five occasions during the Elite player merriments: the Rising Stars Challenge, Abilities Challenge, Three-Point Challenge, Sure thing Challenge, and the Elite player Game.

Lillard began every one of the 82 games for the second consecutive year and arrived at the midpoint of 20.7 places, 5.6 helps and 3.5 bounce back per game. Portland completed fifth in the Western Gathering with a 54-28 record and confronted the Houston Rockets in the principal round of the 2014 NBA end of the season games. In Game 1 of the series, Lillard kept 31 focuses and nine bounce back in his most memorable season finisher appearance to assist with pushing Portland to a 122-120 extra time prevail upon Houston. In Game 6 of the series, Lillard turned into the main player to make a signal beating shot to win a season finisher series since Utah's John Stockton against Houston in 1997. Lillard's 3-pointer as time lapsed gave Portland a 99-98 triumph over Houston, as he wrapped up with 25 focuses to lift the Pioneers to their most memorable season finisher ser es win beginning around 2000. The Pioneers proceeded to lose in five games to the San Antonio Spikes in the subsequent round. Lillard had a series-best game in Game 4 with a 25-point exertion, assisting the Pioneers with dominating their only match of the series. At the season's end, Lillard was named to the All-NBA Third Group..

2014-15 season: First division title

For the third consecutive season, Lillard began each of the 82 games for the Pioneers. He found the middle value of profession highs in focuses, bounce back, takes, and field objective rate, however arrived at the midpoint of a vocation low 34% from three-point range. He shot well during the initial two months of the time, prior to battling with his shot from January onwards. Notwithstanding this, he set the standard for most three-pointers in a player's initial three seasons, drove the group in Win Offers, and completed second in PER. On December 19, 2014, he scored a profession high 43 focuses in a 129-119 triple-extra time prevail upon the San Antonio Prods. After four days, he had a 40-point exertion against the Oklahoma City Thunder.

On January 5, 2015, he had a 39-point exertion against the Los Angeles Lakers. On February 8, 2015, Lillard was chosen as a swap for the harmed Blake Griffin in the 2015 NBA Top pick Game. On Walk 4, 2015, Lillard kept a profession high 18 bounce back in a 98–93 win over the Los Angeles Trimmers. The Pioneers completed the standard season as the fourth seed in the Western Meeting with a 51-31 record. They confronted the Memphis Grizzlies in the primary round of the end of the season games, where they lost in five games. Lillard shot 16% from three-point range during the series, hitting only 5-of-31 remembering going 0-of-6 for Game 1.

2015-16 season: Establishment player

Lillard being protected by Russell Westbrook with the Pioneers in January 2016

On July 9, 2015, Lillard marked a five-year, $120 million agreement expansion with the Pioneers. On October 28, 2015, Lillard kept 21 focuses and 11 aids a season-opening win over the New Orleans Pelicans. His one three-pointer made during the game was his 600th profession three-point field objective, making him the quickest NBA player in history to arrive at the imprint at 247 games. Furthermore, Lillard's 11 helps gave him 1,500 for his profession, making him the quickest Pioneer to arrive at the achievement since Terry Watchman (1987-88 season, 215 games) In the accompanying game on October 30 against the Phoenix Suns, Lillard turned into the quickest player to arrive at 5,000 places and 1,500 helps (248 games) since Derrick Rose (240 games). On December 12, in a misfortune to the New York Knicks, Lillard turned into the principal Overcoat since Clyde Drexler in 1991-92 to record 600 focuses and 150 helps during the group's initial 25 games. On December 21, Lillard missed the primary round of his vocation with plantar fasciitis in his left foot, finishing his dash of playing in 275 back to back games. Backcourt accomplice C. J. McCollum likewise missed the game, leaving the Pioneers without their two driving scorers to confront the Atlanta Falcons, in this way losing the game 106-97. He missed a further six games with the injury, getting back to activity on January 4 against the Memphis Grizzlies and keep 17 focuses and 7 aids a 91-78 misfortune. On January 8, he scored a then season-high 40 focuses in a misfortune to the Brilliant State Fighters. On January 18, in a success over the Washington Wizards, he hit his 2,000th NBA field objective, one of just eight players to arrive at that imprint since he entered the association in 2012-13. On January 26, in a success over the Sacramento Lords, Lillard posted 15 focuses and 13 helps for his tenth twofold of the time, a lifelong high.

On February 19, he scored a vocation high 51 focuses in a 137-105 win over the Brilliant State Champions. He turned into the main player in NBA history to have something like 50 focuses, seven helps and six takes since the take turned into an authority measurement in 1973-74. After two days, he scored 30 focuses against the Utah Jazz, turning into the principal Coat to score something like 30 focuses in four continuous games since Drexler achieved the accomplishment in 1991. He stretched out that streak to five in the group's following game on February 23 against the Brooklyn Nets. Over his initial 300 games in the NBA, Lillard found the middle value of 21.2 places and 6.2

helps per game. Just four different players in NBA history arrived at the midpoint of 21 places and six helps over their initial 300 games: Oscar Robertson (30.2 and 10.3), Nate Archibald (24.5 and 8.4), LeBron James (26.7 and 6.4) and Dwyane Swim (24.0 and 6.4). On Walk 4, he had his subsequent 50-point round of the time in a 117-115 misfortune to the Toronto Raptors. On Walk 8, Lillard had 41 focuses and 11 aids a 116-109 extra time prevail upon the Washington Wizards, recording his fifteenth consecutive game with 20 or more places. He likewise had his 400th help of the time, making him the main Pioneer with 400 or more aids every one of his initial four seasons. In the Pioneers' season finale on April 13 against the

Denver Chunks, Lillard hit his 827th vocation three-pointer, dominating Wesley Matthews' Portland establishment record of 826. Lillard completed the standard season with a normal of 25.1 focuses per game, while C. J. McCollum found the middle value of 20.8 - making them the first backcourt in Quite a while's set of experiences to average at least 20 focuses each. Lillard likewise turned into the third Overcoat to average 25 or more places, joining Drexler and Kiki Vandeweghe. In the 2016 MVP Race, he completed eighth in all out focuses got, scoring 26 brings up of a potential 1310 places. In the wake of overcoming the Los Angeles Trimmers in the primary round of the end of the season games, the Pioneers continued on toward face the Brilliant State Fighters in the subsequent round. In Game 3 of the series, Lillard recorded 40 focuses and 10 helps to assist the Pioneers with winning 120-108, cutting the Champions' benefit in the series to 2-1. The Pioneers proceeded to lose the series in five games.

2016-17 season: Enchantment Johnson Grant

In the Pioneers' season opener on October 25, 2016, Lillard recorded 39 focuses on 13-of-20 shooting, as well as 9 bounce back and 6 aids a 113-104 success over the Utah Jazz. With his most memorable help of the evening, Lillard passed Jim Paxson for 6th on the establishment profession list (2,008). After four days, he scored 37 focuses, including the go on floater with under a second leftover in extra time, to lead the Pioneers to a 115-113 success over the Denver Pieces. With 27 focuses against the Phoenix Suns on November 2, Lillard turned into the primary NBA player to score at least 27 focuses in every one of his group's initial five games since Kobe Bryant in 2005-06. Lillard's 163 focuses in the season's initial five games are the most ridiculously ever by a Jacket to begin a season. After two days, Lillard scored 27 of his season-high 42 focuses in the last part of the Pioneers' 105-95 success over the Dallas Free thinkers. With 38 focuses on November 8 against Phoenix, Lillard had 262 focuses over the initial eight rounds of the time, the most through the initial eight rounds of a season in establishment history. It was additionally the most by a NBA player since Bryant had 264 through the initial eight of every 2009-10. Lillard amassed a group record 695 focuses in the Coats' initial 25 rounds of the time, overshadowing Clyde Drexler's past characteristic of 681 of every 1988.

He proceeded to miss five games between December 26 and January 4 in the wake of hyper-extending his left lower leg against San Antonio on December 23. On January 28 against Brilliant State, Lillard arrived at 8,000 vocation focuses, turning into the eleventh Coat to stir things up around town and joined Michael Jordan and LeBron James as the main three players to arrive at 8,000 places and 2,000 aids their initial five seasons. On Walk 19, Lillard scored a season-high 49 focuses, attached a lifelong high with nine three-pointers, and conveyed the Pioneers past the Miami Intensity, 115-104. On April 3, 2017, he was named Western Meeting Player of the Month for games played in Spring. Behind Lillard, the Pioneers went a NBA-best 13-3 in Spring to flood into eighth spot in the Western Gathering. Lillard positioned third in the NBA in scoring (29.1 ppg) and tied for fourth in three-pointers made (55) to go with 6.0 helps, 4.4 bounce back and 1.44 takes in 16 games. After five days, Lillard scored an establishment record 59 focuses and coordinated his vocation high with nine three-pointers to lead the Pioneers to a 101-86 success over the Jazz. It was Lillard's 27th round of the time with at least 30 places, an establishment high. He likewise turned into the fifth Jacket to score 2,000 or more focuses in a season..

In the wake of being 10 games under .500 at the Elite player break, Lillard assisted the Pioneers to a 18-8 late-season with flooding to acquired them the No. 8 seed in the Western Meeting with a 41-41 record. They confronted the Brilliant State Heroes for the second consecutive year in the end of the season games, this time in the principal round. Portland proceeded to lose the series in a decisive victory notwithstanding Lillard's 34-point exertion in Game 4. For the series, Lillard arrived at the midpoint of 27.8 places, 4.5 bounce back, 3.3 helps and 1.3 takes per game while shooting 43% from the field, 28% from behind the circular segment, and 96% from the free toss line. On May 2, 2017, he was named the beneficiary of the Enchanted Johnson Grant for the 2016-17 season, which respects the player who best joins greatness on the ball court with collaboration and nobility in managing the media and people in general.

2017-18 season: All-NBA First Group choice

Lillard in 2018

On October 28, 2017, in a 114-107 win over the Phoenix Suns, Lillard arrived at the 9,000-point achievement during the second from last quarter. With 402 profession games, Lillard turned into the quickest Overcoat to score 9,000 focuses. On November 15, he had 26 focuses, 11 bounce back and seven aids a 99-94 success over the Orlando Wizardry. During the game, he outperformed Mychal Thompson (9,215 focuses) for eighth on the establishment's unsurpassed scoring pioneers list. On November 27, he scored 32 focuses in a 103-91 win over the New York Knicks. He completed the game on 2,575 profession helps, moving him past Bar Strickland into fourth put on Portland's vocation helps list. Lillard likewise joined Clyde Drexler and Terry Watchman as the main players in establishment history in the best 10 in scoring and top five in helps. On December 9, he tied an establishment record with nine 3-pointers and scored 35 focuses in a 124-117 misfortune to the Houston Rockets. After two days, he scored a then season-high 39 focuses with five 3-pointers in a 111-104 misfortune to the Brilliant State Fighters. Lillard managed a hamstring injury late in December prior to stressing his right calf toward the beginning of January. On January 12, he scored 23 focuses in a 119-113 misfortune to the New Orleans Pelicans. He moved into seventh in establishment history in scoring with 9,753 places, passing Geoff Petrie (9,732). On January 22, Lillard was named Western Gathering Player of the Week for games played January 15-21. It was his fourth vocation Player of the Week gesture. After a day, he was named a Western Meeting Top pick hold.

On February 2, he scored 32 focuses in a 130-105 misfortune to the Toronto Raptors, turning into the quickest player in establishment history to arrive at 10,000 focuses for his vocation. He turned into the eighth player to get 10,000 focuses and 2,500 aids his initial six seasons, joining Michael Jordan, LeBron

James, Larry Bird, Nate Archibald, Pete Maravich, Dave Bing and Oscar Robertson. On February 9, in a 118-100 win over the Sacramento Rulers, Lillard scored a season-high 50 focuses in a short time — the fourth 50-point round of his vocation. He scored 22 calls attention to in the second from last quarter prior to sitting the whole final quarter. He shot 16 of 26 from the field with eight 3-pointers to go with 10-of-10 free tosses. On February 14, he had 44 focuses and eight aids a 123-117 success over the Champions. On February 24, he hit a go on rest up with 0.9 seconds left and wrapped up with a game-high 40 focuses in a 106-104 win over the Suns. Nineteen of his 40 focuses came in the final quarter, as he assisted the Pioneers with energizing from 15 down in the last 7+1/2 minutes. In five games between February 9 and 24, Lillard scored 197 focuses — the most focuses for a Coat more than a five-game stretch in establishment history. Lillard found the middle value of 31.4 focuses per game in February, securing the most noteworthy scoring normal for any month in Portland history. He passed Geoff Petrie's record of 30.4 places in Walk 1971.

On Walk 3 against the Oklahoma City Thunder, Lillard made no less than one 3-pointer in his 45th consecutive game, establishing an establishment standard. With nine helps on Walk 15 against the

Cleveland Cavaliers, Lillard turned into the third player in association history to have 1,500 cr more focuses and 400 or more aids every one of his initial six seasons. On Walk 20 against Houston, Lillard's establishment record dash of 52 games with a 3-pointer finished. In the Pioneers' season finale on April 11, Lillard kept 36 focuses and 10 aids a 102-93 success over the Utah Jazz. The success procured the Pioneers the third seed in the end of the season games with a 49-33 record. Lillard completed the customary season tied for fourth in scoring normal in the NBA (26.9) — Drexler was the last Overcoat to rank among the association's five best in scoring when he completed fourth during the 1991-92 season

(25.0). For the season, he was named to the All-NBA First Group, turning into the third player in establishment history to procure All-NBA First Group praises, joining Clyde Drexler (1991-92) and Bill Walton (1977-78). Furthermore, he set fourth in the 2018 MVP Race, winning 207.0 of the 1010 potential points.In Game 4 of the Pioneers' first-round season finisher series against the Pelicans, Lillard scored 19 focuses in a 131-123 misfortune. The misfortune wiped out Portland from the end of the season games, as they lost the series in a four-game compass. Lillard never scored in excess of 20 in the series and was held underneath that multiple times.

2018-19 season: Western Gathering Finals

Lillard in 2019

In the Pioneers' season opener on October 18, 2018, Lillard scored a game-high 28 focuses in a 128-119 win over the Los Angeles Lakers. On October 25, he scored 34 of his 41 places in the last part of the Pioneers' 128-114 success over the Orlando Sorcery. On October 27, he scored 42 focuses in a 120-111 misfortune to the Miami Intensity, obscuring the 11,000-point mark.On November 16, he had five helps against the Minnesota Timberwolves to pass Damon Stoudamire (3,018) for third in the group's profession list. After two days, he scored 40 focuses in a 119-109 win over the Washington Wizards. On November 28, he scored 41 focuses and set an establishment standard with ten 3-pointers in a 115-112 win over the Wizardry. His seven 3-pointers in the third were an establishment record for a quarter. On December 17, he scored 22 of his 39 places in the second from last quarter of the Pioneers' 131-127 success over the Los Angeles Trimmers. On December 27, he hit a go on 3-pointer with 6.3 seconds left in extra time and scored 21 focuses in a 110-109 win over the Brilliant State Warriors.Two days after the fact, he hit six 3-pointers and scored 40 focuses in a 115-105 misfortune to the Champions. It was his fifth 40-point round of the time, tying a lifelong high. On January 14, in a 115-107 misfortune to the Sacramento Rulers, Lillard scored 35 focuses to turn into the quickest player in Portland history to reach 12,000 for his profession. Moreover, Lillard scored in twofold figures in his 184th successive game, breaking a bind with Clyde Drexler for the establishment record. With 24 focuses against the Phoenix Suns on January 24, Lillard arrived at 1,311 focuses for the season, the most by any Portland player through 50 games.

On Walk 7, he scored a season-high 51 focuses in a 129-121 extra time misfortune to the Oklahoma City Thunder. On Walk 15, he scored 24 focuses in a 122-110 win over the New Orleans Pelicans, turning into the second-driving scorer in establishment history, passing LaMarcus Aldridge (12,562) to sit behind just Drexler (18,040).With 31 focuses and 12 aids a twofold extra time triumph over the Brooklyn Nets on Walk 25, Lillard recorded his twentieth profession round of no less than 30 places and 10 helps, passing Drexler for the most such games in establishment history (19). On April 1, he was named Western Gathering Player of the Week for the week finishing Walk 31, denoting the seventh week by week distinction of his profession and the first of the 2018-19 season. In April, he turned into the primary Jacket to have 2,000 focuses and 500 aids a similar season, and the main Overcoat other than Drexler to arrive at 2,000 places in two seasons with the group. He likewise passed his establishment record of 229 3-pointers set in the 2015-16 season and came to 1,500 for his profession. Lillard put sixth in the 2019 MVP race, getting 69 of the 1,010 accessible places.

On April 23, Lillard hit a 37-foot, game-dominating 3-pointer at the bell and got done with a season finisher vocation high 50 focuses to assist the Pioneers with killing the Roar from the end of the season games in five matches with a 118-115 triumph. He had ten 3-pointers, breaking the establishment record. In Game 1 of the subsequent round, Lillard scored 39 focuses in a 121-113 misfortune to the

Denver Chunks. In Game 6, he scored 32 focuses in a 119-108 win, assisting the Pioneers with tieing the series against the Pieces at 3-3. In the concluding Game 7, he scored 13 focuses on 3-of-17 shooting in a 100-96 win, propelling the Pioneers toward the Western Meeting Finals interestingly beginning around 2000. In Game 2 of the gathering finals, Lillard isolated his ribs, yet kept on playing through the agony until the end of the series — a series the Pioneers lost in a four-game range to the Heroes.

2019-20 season: Vocation high in helps per game
On November 8, 2019, Lillard recorded a then profession high 60 focuses, however it arrived in a

misfortune to the meeting Brooklyn Nets, 115-119. He would outperform that on January 20, 2020, by scoring 61 focuses to oblige 10 bounce back and 7 aids a 129-124 extra time win versus the Brilliant State Fighters. From January 20 through February 1, Lillard had a six-game stretch of averaging 48.8 focuses per game; he likewise recorded his most memorable vocation triple-twofold on January 29 by enrolling 36 focuses, 10 bounce back, and 11 aids a 125-112 triumph over the Houston Rockets. The memorable scoring run acquired him consecutive Western Gathering Player of the Week grants. On January 30, Lillard was chosen to his fifth Elite player gesture however couldn't take part because of a crotch injury. He missed six games from February 21 to Walk 2. Lillard got back to play in the last four Overcoats' games before the NBA break because of the Coronavirus pandemic; during this range, he arrived at the midpoint of 20.8 places, 3.8 bounce back, 6 helps, and 1.8 takes per challenge while shooting 40% from the field, 41.2 percent on 3-pointers, and 87.5 percent at the free-toss line.

On June 30, 2020, Lillard was chosen to be the cover competitor for NBA 2K21. In Portland's fourth game in the Orlando bubble, after getting back from the four-month break, Lillard kept 45 focuses and 12 aids a 125-115 success over the Denver Chunks on August

6. After three days, he would follow that up with a 51-point, 7-help execution to lead the Pioneers to 124-121 triumph over the Philadelphia 76ers. On August 11, Lillard ejected for 61 places, tying a lifelong high, and 8 helps on the way to a 134-131 success over the Dallas Dissidents. This was his third 60-point outing of the time, joining Shrink Chamberlain as the main two players in association history to have such games multiple times in a solitary season. Lillard scored a NBA-high 37.6 focuses and 9.6 aids the air pocket's cultivating games, driving Portland to a 6-2 record. He was casted a ballot the NBA Player of the Cultivating Games. He set eighth in the 2020 season MVP race, getting 23 of the 1,010 accessible places.

2020-21 season: NBA Colleague of the Year

On January 30, 2021, Lillard scored a season-high 44 focuses, close by a game-dominating three at the ringer, in a 123-122 win over the Chicago Bulls. On February 17, 2021, Lillard scored 43 focuses and tied a profession high 16 aids a success against the New Orleans Pelicans. He became one of just 12 players in NBA history to have 40 focuses and 15 aids a game. Lillard put seventh in the 2021 MVP race, getting 38 of the 1,010 accessible places. This noticeable the fifth time in six seasons that he had set among the best 8 in MVP casting a ballot.

During Game 5 of the principal round of the 2021 end of the season games against the Denver Chunks, Lillard scored a season finisher vocation high 55 focuses, behind a NBA season finisher record 12 made three-pointers, as well as 10 helps. Lillard hit game-tying threes close to the furthest limit of guideline and close to the furthest limit of the principal extra time to keep Portland alive; be that as it may, the Chunks energized to a 147-140 twofold additional time triumph to take a 3-2 series lead. In Game 6, he had 29 focuses and 13 helps, yet the Jackets lost to Denver 126-115, sending Portland home in the First Round for the fourth time in quite a while.

2021-22 season: Injury and missing end of the season games

On November 20, 2021, Lillard scored a season-high 39 focuses, alongside 7 helps and 3 blocks, in a 118-111 triumph over the Philadelphia 76ers. On January 13, 2022, he went through a medical procedure for a stomach injury and was precluded 6 two months.

On February 10, Overcoats interval head supervisor Joe Cronin expressed that Lillard would "in all likelihood" not play again during the 2021-22 season. On Walk 21, Lillard was authoritatively precluded until the end of the time. This was the initial time since Lillard's freshman season that Portland missed the end of the season games, completing the season with a 27-55 record.

2022-23 season: Rebound and vocation high in scoring

In the wake of missing the last 47 games last season with wounds, Lillard scored 41 focuses in Portland's second and third rounds of the new season to lead them to a 3-0 beginning. Lillard became one of eight players all-opportunity to score something like 40 focuses two times in his group's initial three rounds of the time, a rundown that incorporates Shrivel

Chamberlain (multiple times) and Michael Jordan (multiple times). In the season opener at Sacramento, Lillard moved into the main 10 all-time three-point field objectives made list. For his play, he was named the NBA Western Gathering Player of the Week for the fourteenth time in his vocation. His 14 Player of the Week praises are the most in Pioneers history. On December 19, Lillard scored 28 focuses in a 123-121 misfortune against the Oklahoma City Thunder, and he outperformed Clyde Drexler (18,040) to turn into the establishment's unsurpassed scoring pioneer.

On January 12, 2023, Lillard scored a then season-high 50 focuses in a 119-113 misfortune against the

Cleveland Cavaliers. It was his fifteenth profession game with at least 50 places. He joined James Solidify and Stephen Curry as the main three players over the beyond 10 seasons with at least 10 50-point games. on January 23, Lillard hit his 2,283rd profession three-pointer, passing Jason Terry for seventh on the NBA's unsurpassed rundown in the Coats' 147-127 against the San Antonio Spikes. In the accompanying game on January 25, Lillard had a season-high 60 focuses, hitting nine 3-pointers, alongside seven bounce back, eight helps and three takes in a 134-124 win over the Utah Jazz. He turned out to be only the fifth player in NBA history to score 60 focuses something like multiple times in the ordinary season, joining a gathering that incorporates Shrivel Chamberlain (32), Kobe Bryant (6), James Solidify (4) and Michael Jordan (4). Lillard likewise turned into the principal player in NBA history with three profession rounds of no less than 60/5/5 and he posted the most elevated genuine shooting rate ever in a 60-point game (.898). Also, he hit his 2,291st vocation three-pointer, outperforming Vince Carter for sixth on the NBA's record-breaking list. On February 2, Lillard recorded his subsequent vocation triple-twofold with 33 places, 10 bounce back, and 11 aids a 125-122 success over the defending champs Brilliant State Heroes. On February 18, Lillard won the Three-Point Challenge. After a day, he scored the game-dominating

3-pointer in the 2023 Elite player Match, giving Group Giannis their most memorable Top pick Game triumph against Group LeBron. On February 26, Lillard scored a vocation high and Overcoats establishment high 71 focuses with a profession high and Coats establishment high 13 three-pointers made alongside six bounce back and six aids a 131-114 success against the Houston Rockets, turning into the eighth player in NBA history to score at least 70 in a solitary game. He likewise has 15 games with at least 50 places, 6th most in NBA history. With his work, Lillard turned into the primary player in NBA history to score in excess of 70 places in less than 40 minutes and the main player on that world class rundown to score 70 beyond 30 years old, and the principal to do as such with at least 10 three-pointers. On Walk 6, Lillard logged his third vocation triple-twofold with 31 places, a season-high 13 bounce back, and 12 aids a 110-104 success over the Detroit Cylinders.

Milwaukee Bucks (2023-present)

On September 27, 2023, Lillard was exchanged to the Milwaukee Bucks as a feature of a three-group exchange that sent Jrue Occasion, Deandre Ayton, Toumani Camara and a 2029 first-round draft pick to the Overcoats, and Grayson Allen, Jusuf Nurkić, Nassir Little, and Keon Johnson to the Phoenix Suns. The

Coats likewise got the privileges to trade first-round draft picks with Milwaukee in 2028 and 2030.

Lillard made his Bucks debut on October 26, 2023 against the Philadelphia 76ers, scoring 39 focuses, an establishment record for a presentation, and snatching eight bounce back in a 118-117 season-opening triumph. As a distinct difference, he would battle vigorously in the following game, scoring only six focuses and going 2-12 on field objectives in a misfortune to the Atlanta Falcons. He would quickly return the following game, setting up 25 focuses, 5 bounce back and 4 aids a success over the Miami Intensity.

PROFESSION MEASUREMENTS

Standard Season:

- Focuses per Game (PPG): Around 24.2

- Helps per Game (APG): Around 6.5

- Bounce back per Game (RPG): Around 4.2

- Takes per Game (SPG): Around 1.0

- Field Objective Rate (FG%): Generally 43.7%

- Three-Point Rate (3P%): Around 36.8%

- Free Toss Rate (FT%): Around 88.9%

Playoffs:

- Focuses per Game (PPG): Around 24.0

- Helps per Game (APG): Around 5.6

- Bounce back per Game (RPG): Around 4.5

- Takes per Game (SPG): Generally 1.0

- Field Objective Rate (FG%): Around 41.1%

- Three-Point Rate (3P%): Roughly 36.8%

- Free Toss Rate (FT%): Generally 88.1%

GRANTS AND RESPECTS

1. **NBA The new hotness (2013):**

   - Lillard had a great new kid on the block season with the Portland Pioneers, procuring him the NBA The new hotness grant.

2. **NBA Elite player Selections:**

   - Damian Lillard has been chosen to numerous NBA Elite player games, exhibiting his predictable greatness on the court.

3. **All-NBA Group Selections:**

   - Lillard has been named to the All-NBA First Group and All-NBA Second Group on different occasions, remembering him as one of the association's top entertainers.

4. **NBA All-Youngster First Group (2013):**

   - As well as winning Thenew hotness, Lillard was named to the NBA All-New kid on the block First Group.

5. **NBA Abilities Challenge Champion (2013):**

   - Lillard won the NBA Abilities Challenge during the Top pick End of the week in 2013, exhibiting his adaptability and range of abilities.

6. **Olympic Gold Award (2016):**

- Lillard won a gold decoration as a feature of the U.S. Men's Ball Group at the 2016 Summer Olympics in Rio de Janeiro.

INDIVIDUAL LIFE

Lillard presenting with fans in July 2012

Lillard wears the pullover number No. 0, delegate for the letter 'O' and his excursion throughout everyday life; from Oakland, to Ogden, then Oregon. Lillard is a Christian; he has a tattoo to his left side arm of Hymns 37:1-3. Lillard's sister, LaNae, went to Lakeridge Secondary School. His sibling Houston, who procured a football grant to Southeast Missouri State in the wake of playing football in the lesser school level at Laney School, is an Indoor Football Association quarterback.

In 2020-21 season, he turned into a colleague of his cousin, Keljin Blevins.

On Walk 29, 2018, Lillard had his most memorable kid, a child named Damian Jr. They live in the princely Portland suburb of West Linn. Lillard laid out a Regard Program to help secondary school kids in the Portland metro region graduate.

In 2012, Lillard marked a long term sponsorship manage Adidas. In 2014, Lillard arranged another agreement with Adidas possibly worth $100 million north of 10 years. Lillard has a mark shoe line with Adidas, the "Adidas Lady". In 2017, Lillard marked a sponsorship manage Powerade, an auxiliary of the Coca-Cola Organization. Lillard likewise has underwriting manages Spalding, Panini, Foot Storage, JBL, Biofreeze and Moda Wellbeing. In 2019, Lillard likewise became one of various NBA players to sign an agreement with Hulu to advance the web-based feature's new mission of adding live games to their collection.

Lillard resuscitated the Never Stress Outing in Brookfield Park after his champion youngster season in 2013. The East Oakland occasion was stopped when he was at age 12.

In 2020, Lillard, alongside long-lasting companion and colleague Brian Sanders, became co-proprietor of a Toyota showroom, presently known as Damian Lillard Toyota, in McMinnville, Oregon.

In January 2021, Lillard had his second and third youngster after his life partner Kay'La Hanson brought forth twins, a little girl named Kali and a child named Kalii. In September 2021, Lillard wedded Hanson.

MUSIC PROFESSION

Lillard is a hip-jump craftsman and rapper by the name of Lady D.O.L.L.A., which represents Different On Levels the Master Permits. He started rapping chiefly to drape out in the vehicle of his cousin Eugene "Child" Vasquez, who moved to Oakland from New York City in the mid 1990s. One more enormous impact on Lillard's rapping was his cousin Brookfield Duece, who had some outcome in the Oakland rap scene.

He began a virtual entertainment pattern called "Four Bar Friday" in which he, and any individual who decides to partake, presents a video of themselves rapping a little section on Instagram each Friday with the hashtag #4BarFriday. In July 2015, he delivered his most memorable full length single, "Officer in the Game", through the web-based music streaming website SoundCloud. On October 21, 2016, Lillard delivered his introduction collection The Letter O. On October 6, 2017, Lillard delivered his subsequent collection Affirmed. Lillard delivered his third collection, Enormous D.O.L.L.A. on August 9, 2019, including visitors Lil Wayne, Mozzy, and Jeremih. He presently has his own record name, First Page Music, which remembers Brookfield Duece for its list. Lillard's single "Kobe", which was delivered in September 2020 and highlights Sneak Homeboy and

Derrick Milano, is important for the soundtrack for NBA 2K21 as a recognition for the late Kobe Bryantt.

DISCOGRAPHY

1. **The Letter O (2016):**

   - Debut studio collection delivered in October 2016.

   - Highlights joint efforts with craftsmen like Lil Wayne, Adolescent, and Jamie Foxx.

   - The collection title addresses Oakland (O), Ogden (O), and Oregon (O), critical spots in Lillard's day to day existence.

2. **Confirmed (2017):**

   - Second studio collection delivered in October 2017.

- Incorporates tracks like "Run It Up" including Lil Wayne and "Switch Sides" highlighting Stanza Simmonds.

3. **Big D.O.L.L.A. (2019):**

   - Third studio collection delivered in August 2019.

   - Highlights specialists like Jeremih, Mozzy, and others.

   - Features Lillard's development and achievement both on and off the ball court.

4. **Different On Levels the Ruler Permitted (2021):**

   - Fourth studio collection delivered in August 2021.

- Exhibits Lillard's expressive abilities and addresses different parts of his life.

- Incorporates tracks like "Him Duncan" and "Weber State."

CONCLUSION

As we wrap the last sections up, the story of Damian Lillard, the Rapper, Humanitarian, and B-ball Genius, uncovers an embroidery woven with versatility, ability, and a persevering quest for greatness. Lillard's story reaches out a long ways past the bounds of the b-ball court, reverberating through the cadence of his sections and the effect of his generous undertakings.

In the domain of ball, Lillard's excursion from the roads of Oakland to the NBA tip top stands as a demonstration of the force of devotion and self-conviction. "Woman Time" isn't one minute at work; it epitomizes a mentality — a pledge to adapt to the situation, to embrace difficulties with unflinching self-restraint, and to carve one's name in the blessed pages of donning history. Each step on the court turns into a note in the ensemble of a vocation set apart by flexibility, administration, and a steadfast craving to make a permanent imprint.

Woman D.O.L.L.A., the modify inner self of Damian Lillard, arises as a craftsman whose melodious ability reflects the validness of his excursion. Through refrains that reverberate with the rhythm of his life, he shares the victories as well as the preliminaries, giving a window into the spirit of a man who involves music as a material to paint the shades of his encounters. The combination of ball and hip-jump, two apparently divergent universes, tracks down congruity in Lillard's story, making an amicable mix that improves his heritage.

Off the court, the humanitarian sections of Lillard's story unfurl as a demonstration of his obligation to having an effect. From upholding for civil rights to putting resources into networks, his effect stretches out past the field's limits. Lillard comprehends the force of impact and uses it to inspire, engage, and make positive change, leaving a persevering through heritage that rises above the measurements of his ball profession.

As we turn the last page, Damian Lillard stands as a ball symbol as well as an image of the endless conceivable outcomes that emerge when energy meets reason. The rapper, giver, and b-ball genius — a trifecta that exemplifies the lavishness of his story — leaves us with a reverberating message: that significance isn't restricted to a particular field yet is an excursion that unfurls across numerous aspects. In Damian Lillard, we find a competitor as well as a Renaissance figure whose effect resounds through the fields of game, music, and social change.

9 798867 268701